VERAISON

A Premarital Education Resource

Independently published
ISBN - 9798618072311

www.thebrimkc.com

Veraison- [noun] A stage in the ripening process of grapes. It is the relatively short period during which the firm, green berries begin to soften and change color.

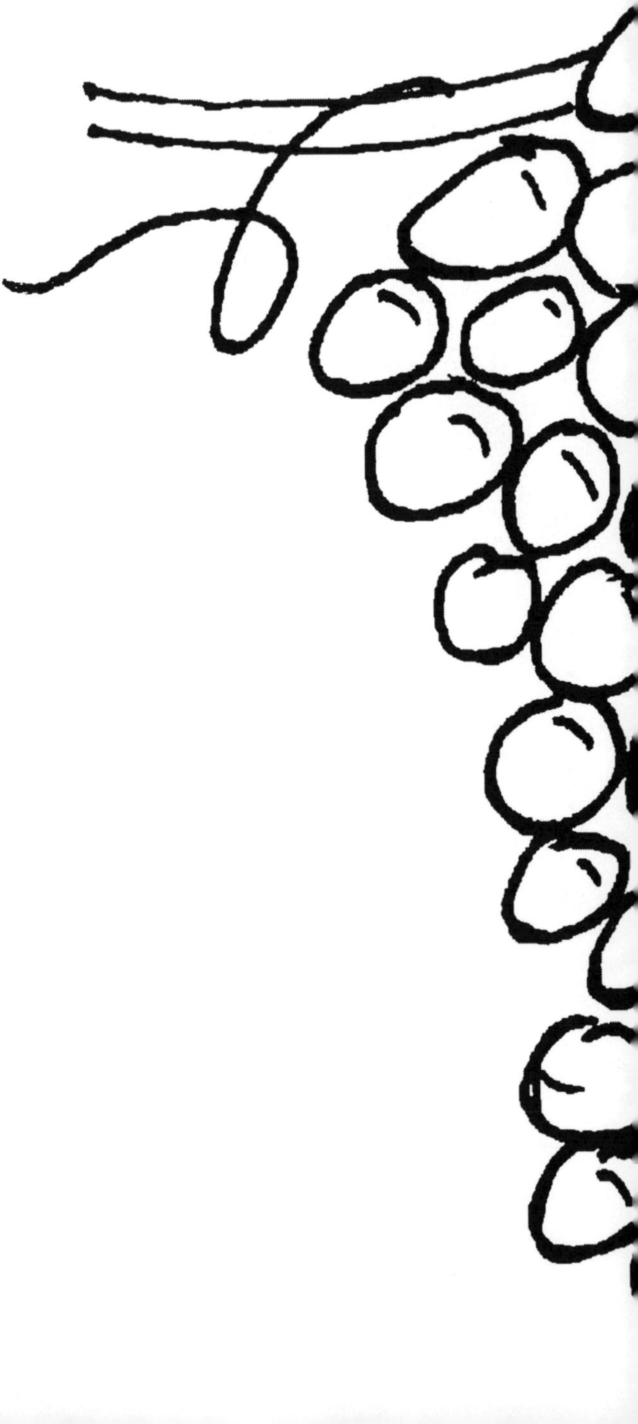

The root of veraison is “ver”, meaning truth.

Foreword

A $100 bill is more than just a piece of paper.
It represents the power to buy goods and services.

Marriage is more than just a piece of paper, too. Marriage represents the power of a partnership that has chosen to become united in the strongest possible way.

Marriage is a limitless commitment, publicly pledged by two people who promise to share... everything. Dreams of hope. Dreams dashed. Tears of joy & laughter. Tears of loss & desolation.

Since Roy and I built our free wedding chapel in 2004, we've had the honor of hosting weddings for many thousands of happy couples. Aaron and Kelsie have likewise built a fabulous wedding chapel as an expression of their faith and their belief in the value of a lifetime commitment.

Sounds scary, right? But the future is coming and it is full of unknown surprises. Some joyous. Some not so much. If you have had the good fortune to find the person you want as your lifelong companion and partner, this workbook is the perfect place to begin your journey.

In the first year of Chapel Dulcinea, I encountered a little boy about 5 years old standing near the bathrooms. He was dressed in a little 3-piece suit with a bowtie and I asked him, "Do you know someone getting married today?" He beamed, "My Mom and Dad are getting married!"

Yes . . . Marriage is more than just a piece of paper.

Newly rooted grapevines require two years to get established.
Newly married couples, too, have lots of things to figure out.

Grapevines need trellises for support.
Married partners need friends for the same reason.

Grapevines need sunlight.
Partners need affirmation.

Neglected vines don't produce much fruit.
Neglected partners don't feel much joy.

Fruit develops only on new growth, so last year's vines must be pruned. Likewise, if happiness is to be always fresh and new, old habits and past grudges must be pruned away.

Well-drained soil prevents root rot, and healthy vines resist destructive pests. Pouring disappointment into the loving embrace of your partner prevents bitterness, and makes you resistant to the charms of others.

First-fruit appears in about 3 years, and full production takes 6 to 8. A committed, considerate couple will be happier in 3 years than they were on their wedding day, and grow happier still with each passing year.

Long-established grapevines produce the richest and most valuable wine.

May your marriage be like wine that grows richer and smoother with each passing year.

To Life!

Pennie Williams,
Joyously married 44 years and counting

Preface

In 2016, I started to kindle an appreciation for the grape: the heritage that it has, the places it has been, and what has been done with it. I started to learn and grow in my knowledge of viticulture and winemaking. I am not a professional in the area; I just have a certain appreciation of it.

As my appreciation of the grape began to grow, Kelsie and I also began to pursue another passion. Before long, we had purchased land, acquired a fifty-year permit, met some wise business owners, met an architect, fixed a bulldozer, put telephone poles in the ground, painted them white, and began to tell a story to anyone who would listen. It is a magnificent story. And before long, we had raised enough money to build a chapel.

What was the passion we were pursuing? Helping brides and grooms have the most successful start to their marriages as possible.

We figured we could help in two ways: give them a beautiful space to get married at the cheapest rate possible, and offer premarital classes to those that are wanting and willing.

And that's why you are reading this. You know your marriage is worth investing in. You won't settle for the statistics of those who came before you. You know there is something to be said about marrying your best friend and being with them forever, so you will do everything in your power to start your marriage off right.

Congratulations.

You are one step ahead. By going through marriage courses before you say "I do", you are raising your marriage success rate, statistically, from 58% to 79%.

Every couple claims, "We will never separate."

I hope you don't, truly. But the numbers are what they are, and have you ever heard a couple, before the wedding say, "We will eventually get a divorce."?

No.

The truth is this, and I know you have heard it before: love is blind.

We are attempting to open our eyes to the hardships and realities of marriage with the hope that we won't miss out on something so good. This is going to be tough. But we must go through these sections, and we must be willing to have the courage to have the hard conversations now.

Are you ready for an adventure?

Aaron Kleinmeyer

In 2011, a boy called and asked me to go to dinner with him. Thinking it was as friends, I told him yes, then realized it was intended to be a date. So I told him no. A year and a half later, I married him.

The funny thing about love is that it doesn't always grow in expected places. It takes root in the small moments, in the everyday, in deep friendships that bloom into an even deeper commitment that isn't always roses and romance- and yet, it's better.

This transformation, this maturity, doesn't take place over night. It is a process, one that is truly never perfected. One that reveals imperfections and weaknesses, selfishness and insecurities. And yet, there is beauty in the process- in growing together, in making the effort to admit wrongdoing and to prune away pride, even when it's hard.

I've stood in dressing rooms and church sanctuaries with brides getting ready to walk down the aisle- the very moment they've been picturing and planning for months, maybe even their entire lives. I can't help hoping that they've spent half of that same creative energy planning and preparing for their marriage- not just their wedding day. Because at the end of that aisle is not only their groom, but also the start of an adventure- full of ups and downs, highs and lows- a great, sanctifying journey that will reveal more about yourself and your new spouse than you could ever dream- the good and the not so good.

So I applaud you. Here you are, starting this process, dipping your toe into something great. Taking the time to invest in something that will last much longer than the 24 hours that make up the day you'll say I do: your marriage. It won't always be easy, but it will always be worth it.

Give each other grace, assume the best intentions, have the hard conversations. Navigate through this guide and never stop fighting for your marriage, rather than for your side.

In 2013, I married my best friend, said yes to dinner dates forever, and never looked back. Our journey is only beginning, but it has already been the most amazing ride. We are far from experts, but together we are learning, growing, and maturing into something much greater than ourselves. And that is what we hope for you as well. Are you ready?

Kelsie Kleinmeyer

Success & Expectations

Stage I, or the cell division phase, is when the berry undergoes rapid cell division, accumulates acids (primarily tartaric and malic), and ultimately achieves half of its final weight and size.

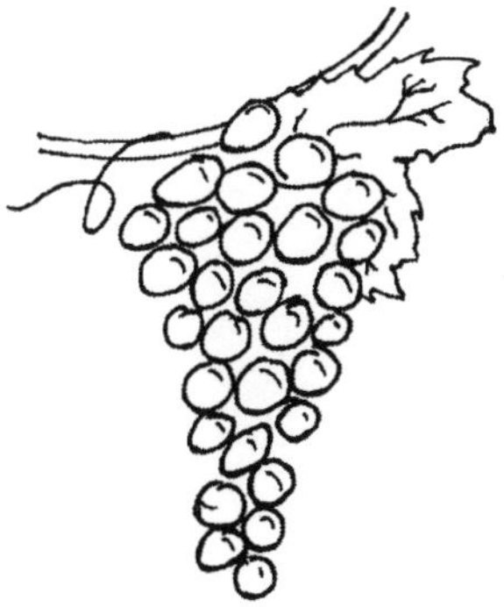

Veraison

A successful marriage is hard to define. However, for many, it starts with making sure each person knows and agrees to clear expectations. If we can go into marriage knowing who takes the trash out, we are less likely to fight and argue. Obviously, this is not an end-all exercise. This is not meant to be used as an instrument for an "I told you so" argument.

At the end of the day, this is an exercise that will make us think and be sure we are ready to see that these items get handled. We do not want to wake up one day to an overflowing trash can with an assumption that someone else was going to handle that. You can see how this can quickly head south for couples.

We would also like to challenge you to not just say, "We will both do it." The fact is, this makes it much harder to actually get things done. And when it's not done, who will be held accountable?

Do you remember the overflowing trash can and kitchen sink when you lived with those roommates? It got done eventually, but not often, and it probably led to some frustration as well.

Be wise and take some ownership.

Let's start by filling out the following chart. Who will do what in your marriage?

Who will:	~~Me~~ Q	~~Them~~ K
Cook/Prep Food		✓
Clean Dishes		✓
Shop for Groceries	✓	✓
Vacuum	✓	
Do Laundry	✓	✓
Maintain Vehicle(s)	✓	
Perform Lawn Care	✓	
Get the Mail	✓	
Take Out the Trash	✓	
Clean the Toilets		✓
Clean the Showers/Tub		✓
Change the Sheets		✓
Clean Out the Fridge		✓
Clean Sinks and Counters	✓	✓
Pay Bills		✓
Handle Plumbers, Electricians, Roofers, Etc...	✓	
Prepare Taxes		✓
Keep the Calendar in Order		✓
Perform House Maintenance	✓	
Put Kids to Bed	✓	✓
Set up Health Appointments		✓
Balance Finances	✓	✓
Discipline Kids	✓	✓

How much will you see each other on a daily basis? A weekly basis? Consider your work schedules.

every morning
every evening
weekends

What does your daily schedule look like?

Will you have weekends off? ________

Will you have days off together? ________

What do you expect those days to look like?

> "After all these years, I see that I was mistaken about Eve in the beginning; it is better to live outside the Garden with her than inside it without her." — **Mark Twain**

Will you be able to eat meals together? yes

Will you eat at a dinner table? coffee table

How often will you eat out per week? once

Does anyone have certain dietary needs/wants and how will that affect the way you eat?

"creatine in my food" Q

How often will you go on dates? once a week

Do either of you snore? we both do

On a scale of 1-10, 10 being most important, how important is it that you sleep in the same bed? 10

Will you have a TV in your bedroom? yes?

How often do you plan to watch TV? ehhh

What type of programming are you interested in?

mystery Adam Sandler
rom coms Will Ferrell

Will you have pets? What types?

cat fishy ducks
dog chickens (basically a farm)

How often do you expect to spend time with your friends on a monthly basis? once a week or every other

Are you comfortable opening your house up to friends? yes

What hobbies do you enjoy?

___

___

> "If I get married, I want to be very married."
> — **Audrey Hepburn**

What hobbies will you do together?

board games

puzzles / legos

cooking

What are your thoughts about alcohol? Are you okay with it being in the home, around kids? Is there a background here that should be discussed?

___

it's fine.

___

___

Where do you plan to live? Lydia Rose

What is the ideal location for you? Think country, suburb, beach, city. country or secluded suburb

Do you plan to own or are you okay with renting?

right now!

Would you rather live in an apartment or house?

right now

What is the highest level of education you have?

Do you plan to go back to school? Give details.

Q → yes – masters

K → no. never.

On May 19th, 2018, Prince Harry and Meghan Markle said "I do" in St George's Chapel at Windsor Castle in the United Kingdom. It was estimated that 1.9 billion people watched the wedding. This is pretty remarkable when you consider that there are around 7.5 billion people on the earth and 1.6 billion do not have easy access to a TV.

What social media accounts do you have?

Q

What are your cell phone, social media, and technology expectations for you and your spouse?

Family & Beliefs

Stage II, or the lag phase, is when berry growth pauses, and the primary focus is on seed growth and chemical signaling to prepare the berry for softening and expansion in the next stage. The duration of the lag phase is variety-specific — varieties with long lag phases tend to be later ripening, while varieties with relatively shorter lag phases ripen earlier.

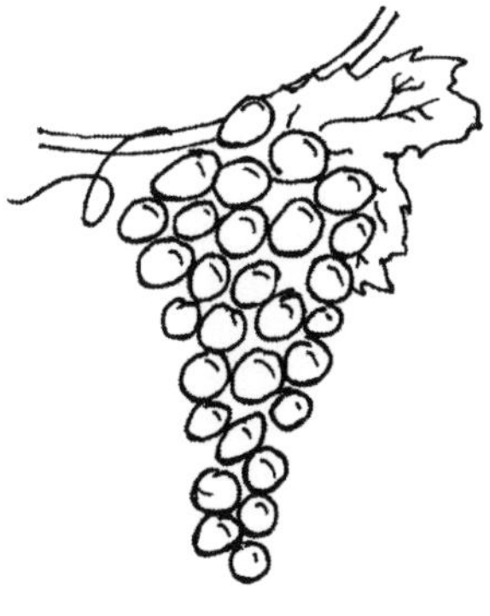

When you tie the knot, it doesn't involve just yourselves. The reality is that two families will come together, they will celebrate you, and in the end, will have to interact to some extent.

We have witnessed this go flawlessly in some cases, and in other cases it can cause a lot of distress between couples. It is certainly worth looking into beforehand.

Your family has morphed your beliefs, the way you do things, and the way you will want to do things. Ultimately, you are starting a new family. The consideration of where you came from and where you are wanting to go is of high regard.

Some of the highest reasons for divorce and marital strife are found in this section. We will be sure to point them out and highlight why.

For now, fill out the questions; don't hold anything back. Be as open and honest as possible. The rest of your emotional life, and that of others, is at stake.

We can't stress this enough. It is worth it though.

Trust us.

Where did you grow up? ______________________________

Who raised you? ______________________________

What is your relationship with them like?

____

____

____

Were they married? Divorced? Never married? And how does this affect your beliefs about marriage?

____

____

____

____

Do your parents live near where you will live? ______

How many siblings do you have? ______

Explain your relationship with them. Are you close to them?

____

____

____

____

____

Did you have any traditions from childhood that you want to keep as an adult? What are they?

____

____

____

What will your holiday celebrations look like? How will you split time? Will you have to travel? Will you try to go to each side every holiday or maybe rotate years? Give this some real thought.

____

____

____

____

____

How much will you spend on the following gifts for family members?

Holiday	Spouse	Siblings	Parents	Friends	Coworkers
Birthdays	50	—	card	50	—
Weddings	—	50	—	50	50
Baby Showers	30 →				

Do you have a relationship with your soon to be in-laws? What does that look like?

____

____

____

____

Are you pleased with this relationship? __________

Do you want children, and how many? 40

Is there any reason you are aware of that might inhibit your ability to have children? Have you worked through this, and what does that mean for you?

____

____

____

When would you like to start having kids?

seatbelts + house :)

Who is going to be more likely to discipline the kids? What types of discipline are you okay with?

____

____

____

Will there be one parent that stays at home when kids come into the picture? If so, explain your thoughts and views on this. How will it change life?

Do you plan to pay for your children's college? If so, how much would you like to save?

People who do not share the same faith or religious beliefs have a 78% divorce rate.

Were you raised in a family with specific religious beliefs? What were they?

What are your current religious beliefs?

____

____

____

On a scale of 1 -10, 10 being the highest, how important is your faith to you? __________

Do you share the same religious beliefs with your soon to be spouse?

____

What are your expectations as far as regularly practicing your faith?

____

____

____

What religious beliefs would you like to raise your children with?

____

____

Money, Conflict Resolution, and Sex

Stage III, or veraison to harvest, is characterized by cell expansion in the berries and a transition from photosynthetic activity to heterotrophic metabolic activity as the berries change color at veraison. In other words, the berries go from being a partial "source" to a large "sink". This sets the stage for accumulation of sugars, proteins, anthocyanins, tannins, and flavor and aroma compounds, and metabolism of acids and an increase in pH. The entire process is brought about by the expression and repression of hundreds of thousands of genes. The changes during this time heavily influence the final quality and composition of the fruit at harvest.

Veraison

Finally, fruit is coming. You have processed through children, history, expectations, and others. Now we will look at how to bind and ensure these fruits stay ripe and fresh.

Certainly, two are better than one. This is especially true when it comes to finances. Our ultimate goal when it comes to money is to be able to place ourselves in a position to freely give to others. Do you have this mindset?

If you are not willing to give some of your money, would you give of your time? Those are your two assets in this life, and one is fixed. Manage them well.

Your time will be spent in a much better manner if you can figure out how to resolve conflicts in a healthy manner. Arguing in marriage is one of the top reasons for divorce. A wise man once told me, "If you go into the argument believing you are right, you are already wrong."

Can we believe this? Are we going to put ourselves in a situation to truly see it from the other person's side? Will we sit down, shut up, and allow ourselves to listen?

Let's find out. Brutally and honestly, fill out the questions.

How much money are you bringing into the marriage?

____

How much equity are you bringing into the marriage? (Think house values, retirement, stocks, etc.)

____

____

____

____

How much debt are you bringing in to the marriage? List out the items below.

____

____

____

____

If you were not getting married, what was your plan to pay these items off?

____

____

____

How does being married affect this debt? Does your soon to be spouse understand this debt?

____

____

____

____

What is your current job? ____________________

What is your expected income each year? _____________

Will you share bank accounts?

____

What amount are you comfortable spending without asking your spouse first?

____

You have a 22% higher chance of divorce if you do not share bank accounts.

Would you consider yourself good at saving money? _________

How many credit cards do you have? And what are your ultimate feelings about credit cards?

____

____

____

____

Do you have any random or unexpected bills you are bringing in to the marriage? What are they?

____

____

____

Who do you expect to handle paying the bills?

____

Dream a little here. What do you want retirement to look like for you and your spouse?

____

____

____

____

____

> "Marry the right person. I'm serious about that. It will make more difference in your life. It will change your aspirations, all kinds of things." – **Warren Buffett**

How will you decide when to bring up difficult topics with your spouse and when to just let them go?

____

____

____

____

How will you lovingly express your frustrations or concerns to your spouse?

____

____

____

____

What sorts of decisions will you make on your own, and which would you ask your spouse about first?

____

____

____

____

When are the best times for you personally to have hard conversations?

____

____

____

Do you believe it is okay to go to bed mad?

____

How can you work to be a better listener?

____

____

____

Are you more likely to "fight" with words or more likely to retreat or get quiet? What about your spouse? How will this need to be navigated?

____

____

____

____

> In an argument, if you believe you are right you are already wrong.
>
> **-Marley Porter**

How often do you expect to have sex?

Who will initiate more often?

Will it be spontaneous, or more planned out?

What form of birth control(s) will you use, and who will be responsible for using it?

Are there any past sexual experiences that you have not discussed with your partner?

Harvest

The Harvest is a special time. You wake up extra early to pick because you know the mid-day sun will beat down and change the sugar content of the grapes. You need your sugar content to remain stable so you have no surprises while the wine is being fermented. You have spent years waiting and now is the time.

Congratulations.

We have included the following pages to encourage you in this new stage of life. This is our harvest.

The first section includes our first seven newsletters. We decided to include them because they were written from a time of new excitement and adventure. We were in the middle of our first season of weddings, heading towards construction of the chapel.

We send these newsletters out to the donors who have made The Brim possible by donating their talents and treasures. These newsletters are full of updates, pictures, and words of encouragement. It is our easy way to say thank you to the folks who have made The Brim possible. We couldn't and still can't do it alone.

The second section contains pieces featured through the years on Kelsie's blog, "Currently, Kelsie". The selections included focus specifically on marriage, and Kelsie's in-the-moment perspective as a new wife and mother. Being picked is just the beginning of the story, and we continue to be refined and renewed over the years. May they encourage you as you do the same.

July 2020

What a unique and special time we are in. Kelsie and I went on a date last week. We have always tried to be intentional about this. And it always leads to our best thinking.

We reflected upon the idea that there would be no better time to enter into this industry than this time we have been given. We also reflected upon what we believe as a business.

Simply put: we believe marriage matters.

But what does that mean?

Kelsey and Drake were left with a decision to make. These two were slated to get married in mid-April at The Brim. But life quickly got turned upside-down in March. It was a Saturday, and the stay-at-home order had been announced to go into effect the coming Tuesday. Kelsie picked up the phone and gave the bride and groom two options. Wait and see what happens, or get married the next Monday. They would need to acquire a marriage license, an officiant, and what about parents and guests?

They chose to go ahead and get married in two days.

Kelsey and Drake woke up Monday morning, got dressed up, and headed off to find a courthouse that would issue them a marriage license. Remember when they were all shutting down? Kelsie helped find an officiant, and we were also able to find a videographer that helped film their ceremony.

We drove to The Brim, not knowing if they had been able to find a marriage license. We set up a few chairs and held our breath. The joy that came over us when Kelsey texted The Brim phone stating they were able to get a marriage license was surreal. This was going to happen.

With the videographer, the officiant, a few friends, and a set of parents onsite, Kelsie and I went back to our truck to watch it unfold. Kelsey's parents were from out of town and were unable to make it with all of the travel restrictions in place. As our first bride was walked down the aisle virtually, with her dad on Facetime, we became emotional.

Out the front window of the truck, we watched the very first Brim Bride choose marriage over wedding.

Given hard circumstances with lots of unknowns, it was a hard decision that had to be made.

Kelsey and Drake headed to a nearby hotel with their group of less than 10 people to enjoy some delivered pizza.

And I drove my own bride home, remembering that marriage matters. You believe this too, right?

Aaron Kleinmeyer

August 2020

Our business model is unlike any other in the industry. We believe marriage matters and that young couples shouldn't have to go into debt to say "I Do."

People are often so confused when we talk to them about how we do free weddings. I get it, at first glance it sounds like a whimsical dream.

It's the perfect idea to ask dream crushing questions to. And trust me, people have tried.

If we are going to say your marriage matters more than your wedding, then we have to have the business model that we have. Where there is absolutely no barrier on our end to come and have a place to get married. For now, our free ceremony includes green grass, a paved aisle, and very special white washed telephone poles. Ask us why the poles are special. From those items, we work up. People have to pay for chairs, tables, linens, arch, tent, extra rental time, etc.

Another key aspect to our business model is that we build and expand within our immediate means. This keeps our overhead extremely low.

From day one, we refused to build an extravagant building because we knew that if we did, we would have astronomical bills to pay. And we would have to charge more to our brides and grooms.

The best is still to come.

Ever since we met some strangers named Roy and Pennie in Texas who introduced us to another stranger that was on their property that day, named Marley, our drive and mission became very focused. Marley is the one who flew to Kansas City and designed the chapel we are going to build. This is a picture of me dropping him and his sweet wife off at the airport.

The weekend he spent in Kansas City is one we will talk about for a long time from now. We sat at a table and watched his hands conceive to paper The Brim Chapel. It was remarkable.

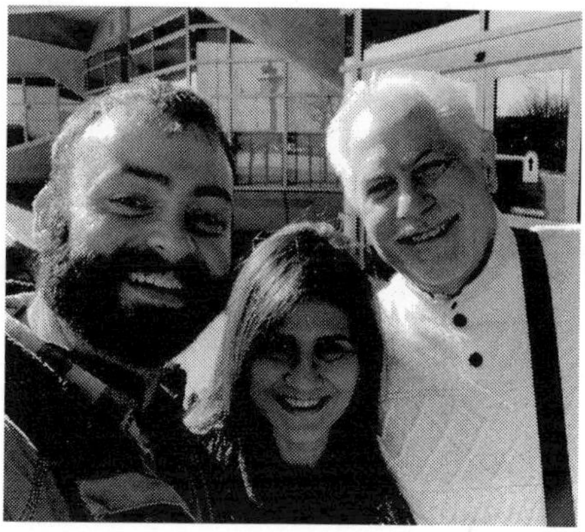

Do you know the full story? It's rather long, book worthy, really.

We will tell it to you if you ask.

For the last year, we have waded into the deep end of the pool to see to it that this chapel keeps moving forward. We have raised over $105K and have about $40K left to raise. We have stomped through the mud to push forward commercial building plans. They are nearly complete, and once they are, I will sit down with our builder and have a potential build date. As I'm writing this, the builder has called and we are working to coordinate building options with the structural engineer.

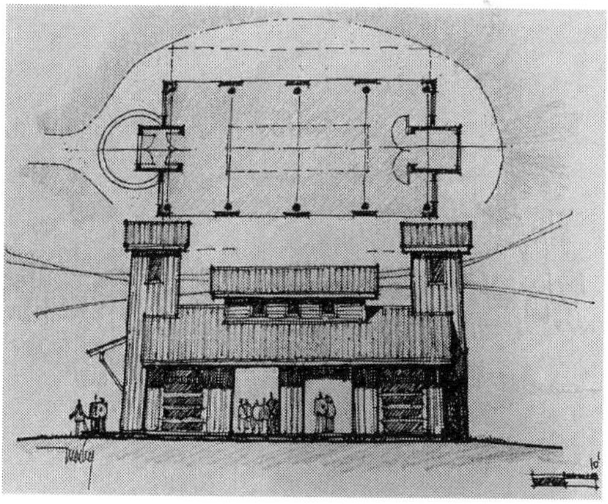

Have you ever built a commercial building? It isn't easy.

But we believe it will be worth it. We plan to offer the chapel for free to brides and grooms forever.

Because marriage matters.

We are heading up a mountain; the view is getting better. Have you seen it up here?

Would you help us finish the climb?

Aaron Kleinmeyer

PS. Did you know around 700 brides in the Kansas City metropolitan area either do not celebrate their wedding or get married at a courthouse each year? Their number one reason for doing so is money.

September 2020

I was holding my son, Eli, who is 3 years old, when I noticed him looking up at some lights and squinting his eyes.

"What are you doing little buddy?"

"Dad, I am making the lights have lines shooting out of them. Do you see the lines?"

It took me a second to realize what was going on. A flood of memories washed over me from my own childhood. I used to do the exact same thing. Make the lights have rays. I also believed that others could see them too.

While I know that others can't see those rays when I squint my eyes, there are new rays I want others to see. Last month I left you with a statistic: 700 weddings happen in Kansas City area every year that are either not celebrated or happen at a courthouse.

I want to dive into another statistic that might be an eye opener. You might have to squint your eyes to see it at first.

I kept hearing about the cost of a wedding over the past five plus years. Every time I would see that statistic, I would be baffled and think to myself, "How can the average wedding possibly cost that much?" I watched the number creep over $35,000 and I had to start doing research for myself.

There are plenty of online giants that do a great job connecting vendors with engaged couples to perform a service at or for their wedding. Every year, some of these sites put out wedding statistics. Brides that go online will see that their wedding, if they want it to be average, will cost around $33,000 this year. What does this do for the average couple trying to get married? My guess is that it makes most folks feel like they simply can't afford to get married.

These online sites are great resource for couples, but we have found a disparity of the perception it has given in the wedding industry. Most of these sites used to be free to list as a vendor.

A lot of people ask, "Why aren't you listed on more wedding websites?"

Our answer is simple, because we would rather put the money it costs to be listed towards free weddings for couples. We also believe advertising is a tax on businesses that aren't remarkable. We believe The Brim is remarkable. Not to mention, very needed in an industry where giants are telling brides and grooms to be ready to spend over $30,000 to have an average wedding.

Is it coincidental that, at about the same time some of these websites started charging vendors to be listed, their claimed average wedding cost hit an all-time high of above $36,000? I'm guessing not. Here is another stat: the average personal income of the bride taking these surveys that drove the average wedding costs statistics was around $60,000 annually.

Veraison

The numbers are skewed. It's that simple. Wedding industry giants have every reason to inflate those numbers. The average wedding is probably closer to $13,000. Dads of daughters, you can breathe a little easier now.

I responded to Eli, "I see the lines! Thanks for reminding me I have to squint to see what is really there."

I hope to never stop squinting.

Do you see the rays?

Aaron Kleinmeyer

October 2020

I sit in agony watching students come up with answers to this question. They genuinely don't know what their answer should be and the reality is that we shouldn't expect them to know the answer. Well-meaning adults fall on this question when they interact with younger folks, not realizing they are falling on a sword.

You see, I thought I wanted to go into the military when I was in middle school; then I thought I wanted to be a mechanic. But "wants" fall short of realities and "wants" often lead to nowhere. There are a lot of things we want, right?

"What do you WANT to be when you grow up?"

Let me save you some time and give you the top answers most students will give if you ask them this question:

- Astronaut
- Veterinarian
- Doctor/Nurse
- Teacher

I'm serious, 90% of students will answer with one of those four answers.

Less than 1% of them will actually follow through.

It's a bad question to ask students. I don't mean to offend you if I have. I know it is a well-meaning question asked by well-meaning adults. However, it typically spawns from the lack of anything else to talk about. The average person will change careers seven times in their lifetime. Not jobs but careers.

I have stopped asking students WHAT they WANT to be when they grow up and I have started asking them WHO they OUGHT to be when they grow up. No really, I do this exercise with students. Pencil and paper. We talk about how life is once and that careers can come and go. We experience freedom and adventure when doing this activity and eyes often light up in ways you would never imagine.

What would happen to marriage if we asked students WHO they OUGHT to be when they get married? If you have a student, have you ever asked them that? It's not too late.

After all, careers will change more than spouses will; at least that is our hope, right?

Right.

Aaron Kleinmeyer

November 2020

I always keep a pen in my pocket. Been doing it for a while now. A couple of folks that I admire mentioned to me that they did it, so I started doing it too. I also typically keep a small notebook in my pocket to write my thoughts in so I can go back to them later.

The number of situations I've been in where the pen has come in handy has been plenty.

You know the situations well, I'm sure. You frantically look around asking,

"Does anyone have a pen?"

The pen I keep in my pocket is a prized possession. It wasn't cheap either. I told myself that if I purchased one that had some value then I wouldn't lose it.

One of the other items that I always have is my wedding ring. I am inspired by that ring often. It's a reminder of the bond and promises I have with Kelsie.

We got to watch thirty-nine couples place rings on their fingers this season. Serendipitous moments indeed.

But it never fails. Before the ceremony someone always asks,

"Who has the rings?"

Often times the best man does, but not always. Maybe another family member or friend might. The rings will sometimes pass to the ringbearer back to the best man, then to the officiant and onward. Ultimately, they always make it to the fingers of the bride and groom during the ceremony.

Once the ceremony is over, the bride, groom, officiants, and witnesses often complete the paperwork to make it official. At The Brim this was typically under the tent at a table, near the bar. Or even at the bar itself. I spent a lot of time behind the bar this season. I would help serve guests and tend to items anyone would need help with.

"Do you happen to have a pen?"

About 10 couples borrowed my pen this season to sign their marriage license.

Last week, Kelsie and entered in to an agreement with the builders who will be building the chapel. We looked over the plans, asked the right questions, and had moments of serendipity.

We couldn't help but think about all of the rings that will be put on fingers, and memories that will be made.

When it was all done, I reached into my pocket, pulled out that pen, and we signed our names on the contract to make it official.

Kansas City will soon have a new wedding chapel.

Kelsie and I will be waiting for those that need a pen.

Aaron Kleinmeyer

December 2020

We have never felt stronger about the journey we are on. We are resting easy that we are right where we are supposed to be and doing exactly what we are supposed to be doing.

Have you ever felt that in life?

Marriage has a lot of moments like this. Recently, for me (this is going to sound cheesy), but I have been thinking about how I get to spend the rest of my life with my wife.

Do you ever think this way about your spouse?

This type of thinking leads me to a couple of thoughts about why forever matters.

Here they are in no particular order:

- Because forever I will focus on the things of joy I see in her.
- Because forever I will dream big with her.
- Because forever I will be sure my children see a father who believes in forever.
- Because forever my mind is at ease.
- Because forever I will show grace unlike any I have ever shown before.

Forever is an interesting concept. When you think of forever do you think about tomorrow? I don't think most people do. They are focused on something far in the future. Something that is almost mystical.

Here comes the serendipitous thinking that has been swirling in my head:

Don't let forever be the ending, let forever be tomorrow.

Follow me here; forever becomes much more valuable when we make tomorrow well-lived. Our marriages become strengthened, and as a result our relationships with friends and families do too.

Because forever I will live well tomorrow.

I think we are right where we are supposed to be.

Aaron Kleinmeyer

PS. Did you know that before COVID was even a thought, our chapel was designed to be open air with 8 garage doors?

Did you also know that well before COVID we believed we were supposed to focus on small intimate weddings?

January 2021

We have been dreaming lately. More than normal. We have seasons like this where ideas come fast and swift. We actually call these dreams opportunities. Because we believe that dreams are just opportunities in disguise.

The dreams you have are more important than you realize.

These speak to who you are. And they are closer to reality than you think.

People are very quick to take a knife to their dreams though.

Folks think their dreams are too big, too crazy, that others might laugh, the list goes on.

A few years ago, Kelsie and I were dreaming together. We were in Napa for our first trip without our first child, Eli. We needed a break and were so excited to just be together by ourselves. Leading up to this trip, Kelsie and I had been asking the question, "What's next?"

This is a loaded question with a huge back story. For now, just know we were looking for something to do with our time that was meaningful.

While in Napa, I found a Groupon for a mud bath at a local spa. We were young and adventurous, so we went. It was an odd experience, but after we were done with the mud portion, they moved us to a small 10' x 10' room.

In this room, they wrapped us up in massive towels; immobilized like burritos we laid on tables on the opposite sides of the room. Scents, light music, and dimmed lights set the scene.

Traumatized by the mud bath and now unable to move, we embraced the moment and were forced to either listen or talk. We stayed in that room for a while, sharing memories and summing up things we had been dreaming about. Midway through the burrito session, Kelsie said something that was magical.

"We should build a place that people could come to. We could have different events, we can do weddings, we could continue to invite people back, and we would be known as the place that invests in people."

In that moment, and I can't explain it fully, but something in my mind knew that this was what we were supposed to do. It felt like a light switch of sorts. I was overly excited but couldn't move because I was wrapped tightly in my towel. Her dream became mine, and we started to peel back the disguise to reveal a massive opportunity.

We set aside what others might think and started sharing our dream with anyone that would listen.

We invested all of our time and finances.

We celebrated small victories and cried during the big ones.

We just knew.

I hope this encourages you to ask, "What's next?"

Let's get to dreaming.

Aaron Kleinmeyer

Currently, Kelsie

On Stories

October 2018

You never know what your story will look like. I was the Sophomore singing on stage at church, and he was the 8th grader in the aisle. And then six years later...

I was the one who said yes and then no to dinner when I realized it was a date. He was the one who didn't give up. I was the one who friend-zoned a guy I was afraid to lose, and he was the one who patiently pursued. And a few months (and a lot more details, tears, prayers, and conversations) later...

I was the one dancing in the rain on a first date, and he was the one holding me close. I was the one falling in love at a distance, and he was the voice I couldn't wait to hear. And a few months later...

I was the one saying yes to the man of my dreams, and he was the one down on his knees asking me for forever. I was the one in the pretty white dress, and he was the one waiting for me at the end of the aisle. And now?

We're the ones building our dreams together, watching with joy and anticipation as our story continues to be written. It's not all sunshine and roses and styled shoot love- it's downright hard sometimes. But man, it sure is good. Better than any story I could have dreamed up for myself. And this is only the beginning.

Just like us, your story is being written: each day another sentence, another purposeful paragraph. It's beautiful and confusing and often excruciatingly slow- every detail emerging just when you think you can't bear to wait any longer. But then a chapter comes together. And it's breathtaking. A hard one closes, and it's refreshing. And a new one begins. I can't wait to see what's next.

With This Ring

April 2019

Seven and a half years ago, Aaron and I vowed ourselves to one another, slipping shiny new rings on each other's fingers while pledging our love in front of friends and family. But vows aren't just something you say one day and then move on from. They're constant: whispered through our actions, cemented in our sacrifices, and renewed as we learn from our mistakes. They're words and truths that keep us grounded and remind us of how we truly feel about each other: even on the days when it all doesn't feel like roses and fireworks. No matter where I am or what I'm doing, when I catch a glimpse of the gorgeous promise glistening on my left ring finger, I'm reminded just what a circular piece of metal can mean: just how much I can, and did, and will continue to commit myself to- with this ring.

If I wrote them today, here's what they'd look like:

With this ring, I promise to love you even on days I don't feel like it. I promise to choose you again and again, each and every day for all of my days. I promise to do my best to ease your burdens in areas I can since you handle so many other things that I can't.

I promise to laugh with you, dream with you, and throw all I have into making this about much more than just us. I promise to listen, and to do my best to understand, even when we both think we're right. I promise to learn and change together, rather than apart, and to always keep fighting for us.

I promise to always hold your hand, to keep you and our marriage a priority even when we have kids, and to never stop dating. I promise to be open and honest with you, even when I'm not quite sure how I really feel (which will happen a lot...sorry). I promise to wipe off your shirt after I'm done crying on it, and to make last minute plans on occasion because spontaneity and adventure keep us fresh- even though I like to plan.

With this ring, I promise to be your best friend, to always assume the best, even when it's easy not to- to stay in my lane and to value your wisdom. We both know things aren't always perfect, but I promise to forgive and forget, to say I'm sorry freely and without reserving my grudges. I promise to kiss you before bed and when I wake up, to do my best to back the car out of the garage without hitting anything, and to remind you to check the important emails out of the thousands within your inbox.

I promise to laugh at your silly jokes, to stay up way too late watching Parks and Rec while you sleep on the couch, and to make you fresh iced tea because I know it's your favorite. I promise to bear your burdens to the best of my ability, to walk by faith and not by sight, and to sit back and marvel at the wondrous story being written in our lives. I promise to be your helper and to stand by your side, even when times get hard and we're forced to navigate through uncharted waters.

With this ring, I promise that my heart is and will always be reserved solely for you. I couldn't live this life with anyone else, and I'd never want to. I promise to love you, no matter the numbers in our bank account, the hairs on your head, or the days we have left together. You're it, forever. Thank you for loving me and pursuing me in a way I never knew someone could, regardless of my many faults. I love you. Thank you for choosing me to be your bride, today and every day. Because this ring, and these vows- they aren't just for one day. They're forever.

What We've Got to Stop Telling Young Married People

March 2016

The moment you get engaged, people are swarming with a variety of advice. From "never go to bed angry" to "your wife is always right", people have a lot of words to share with others who are about to tie the knot. And, like any wife-to-be, I listened when people shared these words with me. I respected people's life experiences and wisdom, and knew that they had much more experience being married than I did. But there was one statement that came up every now and then that made me feel a little odd. And I kept hearing it throughout our first couple of years of marriage. Even now, I still hear it occasionally. It was never directly stated, but rather implied. And it's something we've got to stop telling young married couples.

We've got to stop telling them that marriage stinks: that it will only go downhill from here.

That they're going to fall out of love. That they are just going through a stage and that they won't care for their spouse after a little while. That their marriage will become an inconvenience that they're annoyed by.

We've got to stop telling them, "Oh, you're still newlyweds." or "Wait until you have kids." or "Someday you won't feel that way about them."

And while those implications may very well be true for some people in some marriages, why should we push those thoughts onto people who are just journeying into marriage? How does that provide them with hope and the opportunity for growth, set them up for success, or make them feel supported? It doesn't.

Yes, things change over time. Marriage can be hard. Stages of live bring new challenges and competition for our time and energy. Life will change, and so will every husband, wife, and their marriage. But they can change together. Just because they've been married for ten plus years doesn't mean they won't like each other any more. Just because they have babies doesn't mean they suddenly won't care about the one they fell in love with. These statements may be true for some marriages, but we don't need to interject them upon couples who are madly in love and just starting out. What sort of hope are we giving folks embarking on the adventure of marriage when we essentially tell them they're doomed from the start? I've seen first-hand several marriages that go against these assumptions, so why not strive for those types of relationships and work together to support and create a healthy, thriving marriage?

So what can we tell people just starting out in marriage?
We can be real. We can tell them it won't be easy, that it will require more grace, patience, and forgiveness than they could ever imagine. That they will learn more about themselves than they ever thought possible, and that they will have moments where they are at their lowest. That there may be seasons where they're frustrated, or where the butterflies go into hiding for a while.

But there will also be times of joy. Of happiness, of confidence that doesn't have to go away, of holding each other's hand for the rest of their lives. Every couple is different, but every couple deserves the chance to succeed. They deserve the chance to be cheered on, supported, and encouraged by others. They deserve to be told, "Hey, I love that you guys are still so in love" instead of "Hey, just wait until later. That will go away."

I've felt at times like people have written off Aaron and I's love for each other as something that will fade, something that is not the norm, something that is in some way not valid enough to last. I've never felt like people were directly saying our marriage would end, but rather that I will dislike my husband someday, or that he won't love me. Yes, we all have our moments. But it's hard to hear people assume that. Especially when we are working to keep our marriage healthy and strong. We are navigating through changes and choices with faith as the center of our marriage. We're happy. And we're grateful to have wonderful friends and family cheering us on. All married couples deserve that chance.

So let's build each other up in marriage.
Let's surround and support our married friends and newly engaged couples. Let's be real, and share our struggles with each other in trusted friendships and relationships when needed. But let's stop telling young married couples that marriage stinks. Let's stop setting the timer on their love and just waiting for them to become "unhappily married ever after". Let's celebrate and encourage them through changes and stages of life. Let's help them succeed.

Why I'm Still Dating My Husband

August 2015

Early in our relationship, we had a serious discussion (well, lots of them actually). But one that particularly stuck out in my mind was this: that no matter how long we had been together, how many kids we had, or how many years we had been married, we always wanted to date.

Now, obviously, some things would change. Aaron wouldn't necessarily be coming to pick me up from my apartment or dropping me off at home in the evenings. But there would still be flowers, surprises, and intentional time spent together with just the two of us. Honestly, dating each other when you're married is the best: there aren't the awkward what ifs or trying to impress someone- you're already committed till death do you part. And after a little more than two years of marriage, dating forever is still our intention. Here are some reasons why my husband and I are still dating:

We're still changing.

We want to continue to get to know each other as we age and grow together. We don't want to wake up one morning, look at each other, and wonder who that person beside us is.

We are choosing to love each other on a daily basis.

If you're married, you know there are days that you still love each other, but are incredibly frustrated with one another. The butterflies and warm fuzzies aren't always there when the laundry is piled on the bedroom floor or when your communication is off. But, regardless of all of that, you can choose to love each other. And it is a choice, every single day.

We're committed to keeping our love alive.

We recognize that the best kinds of love are those that come with true commitment, no matter what. If we are truly striving to love well, then we will show grace to each other daily, and choose to always make the decision that is best for our relationship, and for our love. A fire can't die if it is continually fed.

We recognize that we need time alone without distractions.

Oh boy, is life crazy. There are so many good things to devote our time to, including our jobs, our dreams, and parenting. But Aaron and I both recognize that there are times in which we really need some alone time together. And thus- date nights! If we go too long without some alone time, we both feel it. So we try to regularly "schedule" time together.

We consider our marriage to be one worth fighting for and investing in.

Although there are definitely some reasons for failed marriages that are beyond a spouse's control, we believe that a marriage we are both invested in and fighting for is more likely to last. We recognize that there will be trials and even attacks on our marriage in a variety of areas, but we know that at the end of the day, we are both committed to each other, and we will do whatever it takes to keep it together.

We genuinely love spending time together.

When you're married to your best friend, who wouldn't want to spend time together? It's a no brainer. It's just that much sweeter when you're also in love. I can't imagine life without my sweet husband, and we have the absolute best time on our date nights, even if they aren't fancy, expensive, or even planned.

We want our marriage to be strong for our kids.

We both agree that our marriage needs to come before our kids or else it won't be strong enough to support and raise them. We know that there will be a time that our kids will be grown and on their own, and we still want to recognize and know each other. We will love them deeply, but we don't plan to let them become our first and only priority.

We need time away from the stresses of the world.

Sometimes we all just need a chance to take a timeout, a breather of sorts. We need to forget about stress or conflict or money or responsibility and just have a good time. Date nights are the perfect solution for this- an escape with a best friend that is fun and also strengthens our marriage.

Now, you may be thinking: those all sound like great reasons to date my spouse. But how do I make it happen? You're in luck. Here are some of our favorite ways to keep dating each other:

- Try something new together.
- Make dating a priority (schedule it if need be).
- Be spontaneous.
- Don't be too cool to be kids together.
- Go on at least one trip a year without any family, friends, or kids (even if it's just to a hotel in your hometown).

- Dance together (in the rain, on the street, at the gym, at a wedding, wherever).
- Go on adventures, both big and small.
- Write each other notes and hide them in a lunchbox, purse, or around your house.
- Take turns doing something that your spouse really enjoys (even if you don't).
- Surprise your spouse with tickets to an event, or a surprise planned date night.
- Always kiss each other goodbye and goodnight.
- Hold hands in public.
- Brag on your spouse around your friends and family.
- Give your spouse a completely unexpected gift, just because. (Bonus points if it's something you make).
- TURN OFF YOUR PHONES and just be together.
- Have a candlelight dinner at home.

These are some of our favorite suggestions. Find what works best for you! Your marriage is something worth fighting for. Always assume you have each other's best interests at heart, and show each other grace again and again, over and over. Dating your spouse is one of the very best ways to ensure that you grow together, and not apart.

5 Things That Surprised Me About Marriage

June 2016

Marriage is one of the hardest, most wonderful adventures I've ever been on. The last three years have been the best of my life, and I would marry Aaron again in a heartbeat. He challenges me and cherishes me in the most amazing way that makes me fall in love with him all over again. But I'd be lying if I didn't say this: from the moment you say I do, life is never the same. Two people merging their lives into one is an incredible process, and there are bound to be misunderstandings, differences, and some surprises along the way. Here are five things that have surprised me about marriage, along with what you should do about them.

1. You'll realize how selfish you are.

Boy oh boy, is this a biggie! I never considered myself to be a super selfish person, but once you get married you are aware of just how much your world revolves around you. Suddenly the plans for the day, expectations for holidays, or even what you want for dinner involve another person. It's easy to want your way and to try to take charge, but there are other feelings and opinions to consider.

What to Do About It:

Don't just assume that things will happen a certain way, especially your way. Talk about them. Ask questions. Come to compromises and figure out plans together. Just because you're married doesn't mean you have to give up your own individual hobbies or passions (see number two), but it DOES mean that you need to keep your spouse's needs and wants in consideration. If you work to out serve one another, and put each other's needs first, then you'll be just fine. And when you do have selfish moments, and you will, apologize and make a change for next time.

2. You may not do every single thing together, and that's okay.
As some of you may already know, I'm a huge extrovert. I love to be outside, work out, and be around people. But my husband can only do "extrovert" things for so long. He doesn't recharge with people around, like I do. He recharges with some TV time or even just sitting and relaxing (without conversation). For a while, I thought he needed to be running, outside, and with people- just like me. But then I realized that while we have much in common (music, our faith, teaching, loving sports, etc), there are still things that make us different. And that's amazing! So it's okay if I go for a run by myself, or if he works on cars and watches some TV on his own. Because that's how we recharge.

What to Do About It:
Talk through this. Make sure that you are aware of each other's individual needs, and be real about the solo or "friend" time you'll need. You're still people with unique personalities and passions, and as spouses it is our job to cheer on each other in those passions- even if it's from the sidelines. Don't be upset or feel unloved if your spouse spends time doing their own thing every now and then- it doesn't mean that they don't love you. And if you are truly interested in being a part of your spouse's passions too, then say it! Don't be silent and angry- communicate, communicate, communicate.

3. You've got to learn to speak your mind (with kindness).
I know this one seems kind of obvious, but it's actually trickier than you think- especially for women. Coming from the dating world into marriage means that we've got to flip the switch from being reserved and nervous about what our significant others will think into being totally honest. That doesn't mean we just blurt out our emotions right away in the middle of an argument, but instead that we give our spouse our honest opinion when they ask for it, or tell them what we're thinking when they can't guess it.

What to Do About It:

Always assume the best in your spouse, and give them a reason to assume the best in you as well. If you're struggling with something, tell them. If you're scared about something, tell them. Marriage involves you both, and when things go unsaid then feelings get hurt, expectations go unmet, and confusion appears. Speak thoughtfully, and with kindness. And often. Communication is key.

4. You will have conflict, and that's okay.

In a perfect world, married folks would never have any sort of disagreement. But because marriage involves two imperfect people, there is bound to be conflict. You'll fester over dirty clothes that are left on the floor, or he'll be annoyed that you change your outfit four times before you leave. Sometimes arguments will be quick and loud, and other times they'll go unspoken for days. But guess what- this is normal! You are not the only married folks in the world who have ever had an argument. That's far from the truth. Now obviously if things are getting abusive or if you are regularly struggling with conflict at a high level, you may want to reach out for help or see a counselor (which is also perfectly okay!) But for the most part, don't assume that your marriage is a failure or strange just because you don't always agree on everything.

What to Do About It:

Be real. Figure out the heart of the matter, and examine your heart. Be sure to take responsibility for what you have done and can change. Decide on your action steps to change things, set goals, and put your plans in motion.

5. You're going to keep changing.

For some reason, I had it in my head that once I got married, I would stay the same Kelsie forever and we'd just ride off into the sunset together. While parts of me have stayed the same, I've also seen a lot of change in myself over the last few years. If we're honest, everyone is changing- all the time. We are constantly being shaped by our experiences, hopes, dreams, failures, and successes. This isn't a bad thing, it's just something that we have to be aware of.

What to Do About It:

If we're going to change, we can either change together or separately. Aaron and I are committed to making our marriage work, and so we make an effort to change together. We will be different in five, ten, and fifteen years, but we want to continue to know and love each other, in the midst of all our flaws and failures. Because of this, we're still dating. Share your hearts. Share your words. Continue to know and love each other through all life brings your way!

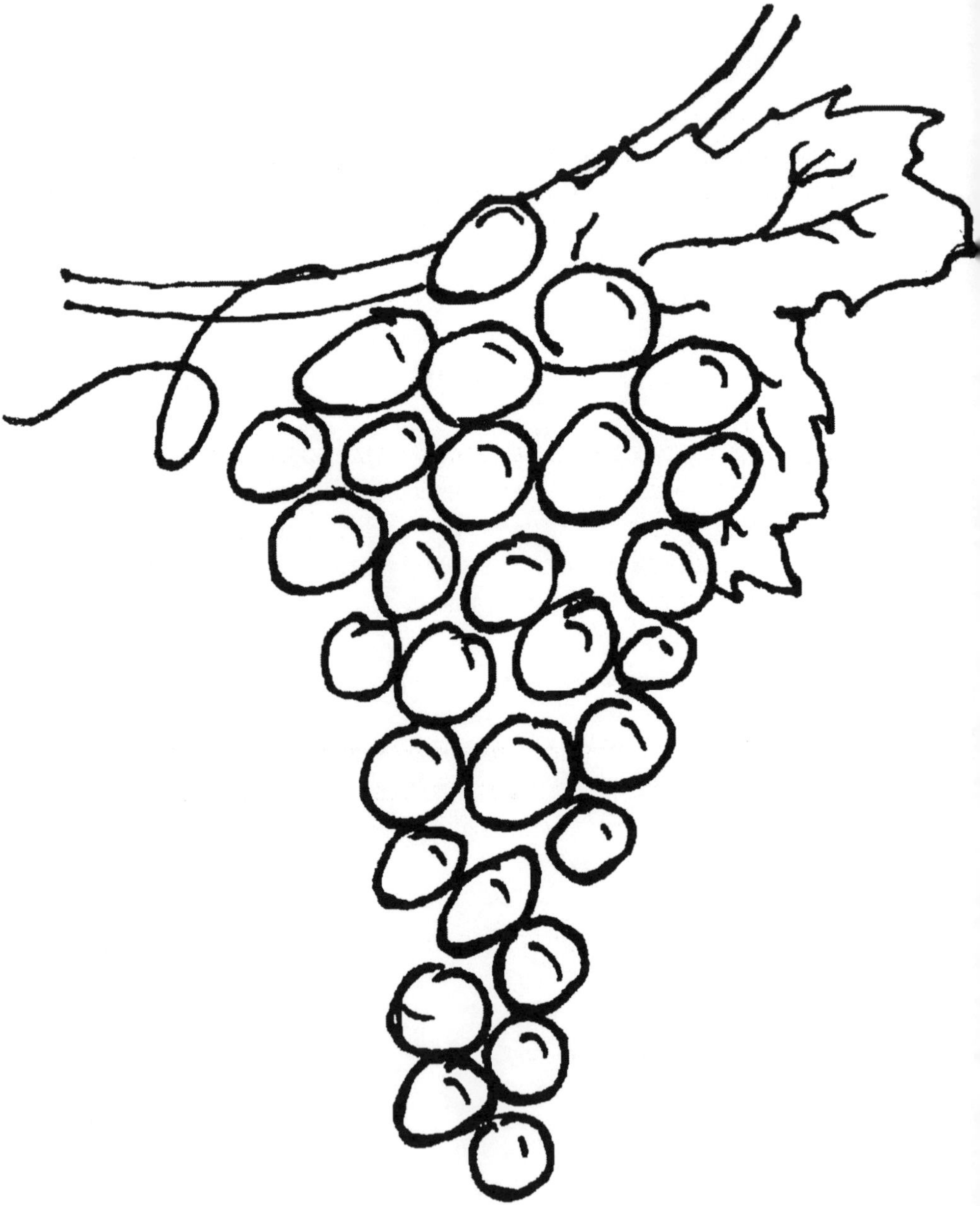

This book is not magical. It will not solve issues between two people. It will only politely ask the questions that might shine a light on compatibility and, if you are lucky, save you from heartache and lead you towards great adventure.

Do you want adventure?

We love adventure, We can attest it makes marriage worth it.

You are staring at your travel ticket. The ticket has a spot for two names. The first name is already printed: it is your name. Next to that, the second line is blank. The real magic is found with you, your story, and the name you are willing to pick and write on that ticket in the blank space.

It's a joyous thing to be picked.

For years, the grape vine is tended to and molded to the trellis before the first grapes are allowed to grow. When the time comes to pick the finest grapes off the vine, it feels like a mountain has been climbed.

But do you know what happens once the grapes are picked from the vines?

Are you ready for an adventure?

Photos

Cover Photo & Pg. 37: A picture of the first block of grapes planted at The Brim during their first year of growth.
(Credit: Haili Wise Photography)

Pg. 31: This is a photo of the first couple that got married at The Brim. The ground were not finished, plenty of brown dirt, right before the Covid stay-at-home order started. (Credit: Jeannette Howard Photography)

Pg. 33: Marley, the architect, and his wife Margarita, came to Kansas City, toured the property, then went back to his hotel to sleep for the night.

Pg. 33 & 34: Marley wakes up the next day. While sitting in a local hotel, the vision of the chapel comes to life. These are the drawings Marley came up with. We loved them.

Pg. 36: A picture from one of the first styled shoots held at The Brim.
(Credit: Haili Wise Photography)

Pg. 38: This sign was displayed at the beginning of the path that led to Founder's Square. We wanted to give everyone a chance to be a part of what was happening.

Pg. 39: Aerial photo of the setup of our first weddings. The tent was 20'x40'. After using that a handful of times, we invested in a tent three times that size. (Credit: Cub Bear Creative)

Pg. 40: This is a photo of the entry to our larger tent, taken during our first Full Friday event for brides and donors.

Pg. 41: We were working during one of the weddings. This was how we would take a short break to eat dinner before getting back to serving the wedding guests.

Pg. 42: This is a picture of the sign we handmade that sits at the entry to our driveway. Yes, we made it.
(Credit: Staci Ann Moore Photography)

Pg. 43: We took this selfie right after we officially signed the documents with the chapel builders.

Pg. 45: This is a rendering of the chapel. This picture became famous on the internet. People kept contacting us wanting to see the building because the rendering looked so real. We hated telling them it wasn't built just yet.

Pg. 47: This is a picture of Founder's Square while it was still under construction. There was no grass, just white poles and a partially finished aisle. (Credit: Kaylee Hoeflicker Photography)

Pg. 51: This is a picture from when we were models in a styled shoot. (Credit: Lacey Rene Studios)

Pg. 52: This is a photo from our engagement.

Pg. 53: A picture of our rings taken in the sanctuary on the morning we got married.

Pg. 56: We had a photo session in a local small town. (Credit: Lacey Rene Studios)

Pg. 57: We love to go to Art Fairs and dream about the art we can't afford. Maybe one day.

Pg. 58: This was taken at Kelsie's 25th birthday party. The theme was "Roaring 20s" and everyone dressed up as their favorite decade. She was obviously 20s; what decade was I?

Pg. 60: Early in our marriage, we went on a cruise. During one of the dinners, they came by and took a picture of us. We couldn't afford the print of the photo. But when no one was looking, we took a picture of the picture. Shhhhh... Don't tell.

Back Cover: Family photo on The Brim driveway. October 2020. (Credit: Lala Inspired Photography)

Veraison

Notes

Veraison

Notes

Veraison

Notes

Marriage Matters

the

BRIM

Living life full

www.thebrimkc.com

To learn more about the classes and events we offer to engaged and married couples, visit our website at www.thebrimkc.com.

Also, if you are interested in helping us continue to write this story, we would love to hear from you. We can't provide free and affordable weddings and educational classes without the help of those who believe in what we are doing.